I.K. Rose

Happy Valentine's Day!

¡Feliz día de San Valentín!

Betty's first English-Spanish Valentine

It's February. The day is cold, but the heart of a little sheep Betty is warm and cheerful.

Today is a special day, it's Valentine's Day!

Betty waited for the day for so long!

Every year she prepares beautiful cards and gives them to her family and friends.

She knows that heartfelt wishes bring lots of happiness.

Finally, Valentine's Day has come!

In the morning Betty gives the valentines to her mommy and daddy.

They hug and kiss her fondly.

Betty also prepared cards for her best friends Bunny Fluffy, Donkey Boo Boo.... and Goat Molly.

She receives colorful valentines from her friends, too! It's so kind!

But that's not the end of nice presents... Today mommy has a surprise for her daughter!

- "Betty my dear, I have a message for you! You received a letter! It's from your distant cousin Penelope!"

It was the first time Betty has received a real letter! She couldn't wait to open it!

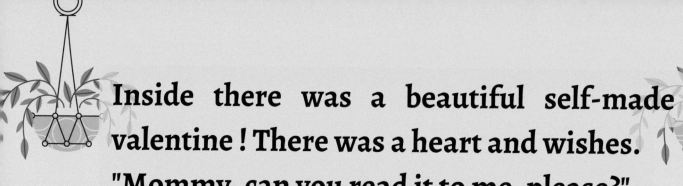

Inside there was a beautiful self-made valentine ! There was a heart and wishes. "Mommy, can you read it to me, please?" - Betty asks.

" ¡Feliz día de San
Valentín!
Abrazos y besos,
Penelope"

Betty looks at mommy, at the card, and mommy again, and says sadly:

"Mommy, the card is so lovely, but I don't understand it."

"Oh, my dear, it's in Spanish!"

"In Spanish? What is written there?" - Betty asks.

"It's written: *"Happy Valentines Day! Hugs and kisses, Penelope!"* - mommy explains.

"I want to write back to Penelope..... in Spanish!" she decides.

"That's a great idea!" - mommy answers.

"I can help you. I know Spanish." - mommy continues. - "I used to visit Penelope's mother often when we were children. We played a lot, and I learned a little Spanish then."

"Now we can learn it together!" - mommy adds.

"I'd love to!" - Betty says happily. -"So let's make a valentine ...in Spanish!" - she adds joyfully.

Betty goes with mommy to Betty's room.

She prepares all the necessary things:

colored cardboard

glue

scissors

crayons

felt-tip pens

When everything is ready
Betty draws and mommy writes:

 heart $\longrightarrow$ el corazón

 cupid - $\longrightarrow$ el Cupido

 rose $\longrightarrow$ la rosa

 gift $\longrightarrow$ el regalo

 kiss $\longrightarrow$ el beso

 chocolate $\longrightarrow$ el chocolate

 candy $\longrightarrow$ el dulce

 bouquet $\longrightarrow$ el ramo

Betty wants to write something more. She asks mommy:

"How to say Spanish...:

Mommy writes:

"I love you"

→ "Te quiero"

"I miss you"

→ "Te echo de menos"

"Hugs to you!"

→ "¡Abrazoz para ti!"

The valentine is ready.

"Thank you, mommy! We've made a wonderful valentine! I hope Penelope will like it..."- Betty wonders.

"I'm sure she will!"- mommy answers - "Now we can go to the post office and send the card. " - she adds.

Betty goes with mommy to the post office. They send Betty's first valentine.... in Spanish! Betty is so happy!

"I'm proud of you that you decided to write back to Penelope and learn some Spanish." - mommy praises Betty.

Betty feels very proud of herself, too!

On their way home Betty says:

"I hope that one day I'll talk to Penelope in Spanish."

"I think it's possible." - mommy replies. - "We may invite Penelope and aunt Maria here, or even visit your cousin in Spain in the summer. "

- "I'd love to!" - Betty answers cheerfully.

Mommy continues: "If we practice Spanish regularly, a little every day, soon you will be able to talk to Penelope! Learning Spanish is a perfect way to start a new adventure!"

"I love adventures!" - Betty smiles.

"And I love you!" - mommy replies.

They both laugh and happy come back home.

Glossary:

¡Feliz día de San Valentín! → Happy St. Valentines Day!

¡Abrazos y besos! → Hugs and kisses!

Te quiero → I love you

Te echo de menos → I miss you

¡Abrazoz para ti! → Hugs to you!

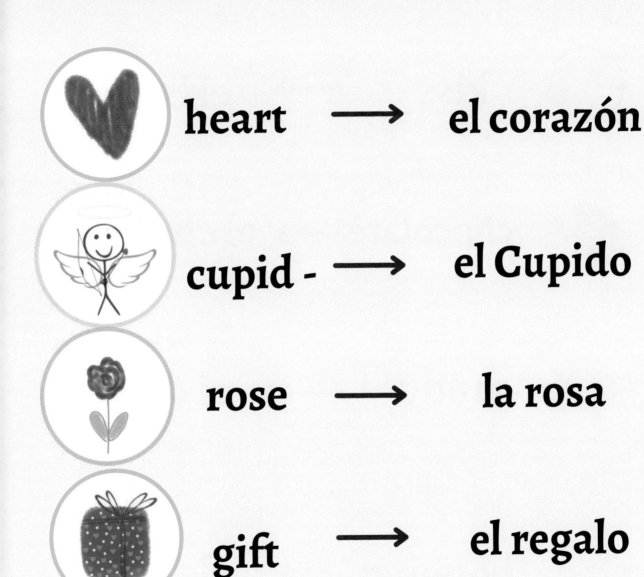

heart → el corazón

cupid → el Cupido

rose → la rosa

gift → el regalo

 kiss ⟶ el beso

 chocolate ⟶ el chocolate

 candy ⟶ el dulce

 bouquet ⟶ el ramo

Goodbye!
¡Adiós!

That is how Betty started her little English-Spanish adventure. This will be a precious journey with small steps which lead to great results.

To be continued...

Teaching tips for parents:

- be supportive
- create a positive learning atmosphere
- use body language and gestures
- change the tone of your voice
- try to "talk twice", first in your native language, then in a foreign language
- repeat often, but shorty, up to 5 words every day
- never put pressure on your child
- play with your child, make it fun

Made in the USA
Columbia, SC
29 November 2024